REVIEWS

TRUE

Top story

Gloriously, madly enjoyable

courage should be admired

Book of the week

A fire fly's

DIARY

By La Fille du régiment

A fire fly's DIARY
By La Fille du régiment

Written and Illustrated by
Gwendolyn Holbrow

ISBN-13: 978-0692633670
ISBN-10: 0692633677

Library of Congress Control Number: 2016902381

Published by Big Sister and the Holding Company
Framingham, Massachusetts

Printed in U.S.A.

Author photo by Charles H. Holbrow

This is a true story.

Dedication

This slender volume was digitized and reformatted for print from the original artist's book created some years previously in Ham, Richmond, Surrey, UK, with the newspapers, library paste, colored paper and hospitality of the author's dear friend, Anna Michel, who would consider that to be "coloured" paper, and to whom this book is dedicated.

TODAY

a little frazzled.

Frosty

DAY

Today QUITE SIMPLY A STRANGE DAY

sensitive day

Dazzled by headlights

ON THIS DAY...

problems

CAN'T FORGET THE weekend

PURE FOLLY

ILL?

serious
illness

FAILING

found out The remedy

I need a break

need light

THIS WEEK

played in the sun

Today

LOTS OF CHOICES

CONSIDER THEM CAREFULLY

On the one hand

On the other,

stupid day

TOMORROW RACING DAY

gripping action

chance

Terror

Sky

Sky

Sky

unforgettable day

YESTERDAY

JUST PERFECT

all this week   precious

TODAY

peace of
mind

CELEBRATE

THE DAY

AND
THE

night

until
Dawn

About the Author

La Fille du régiment is a member
of the Photinus branch of the
Lampyridae family. She enjoys
writing, collage, glowing, and
racing with other fireflies,
especially over dark meadows on
warm humid summer nights.

About the Other Author

Gwendolyn Holbrow is an artist, writer, musician, proud mother of four astonishing human beings, and fortunate wife of a fifth. She sings and plays upright bass in the bluegrass band Moonshine Alley.

About this Book

A fire fly's DIARY emerged into being of its own volition, driven by the imperative of the narrative itself and the choices imposed by the materials at hand. I discovered the diary of a bright little insect, La Fille du régiment, in which she describes the loss and recovery of her glow. Only when she realizes she must have rest and light, and play in the sun, can she recover, summon the courage needed to take creative risks, and again take pleasure in the activities she loves.

A few years later, in the midst of the journey of my life, I found myself in a dark wood wandering, and the straight way was lost. After finding my path home, I came across this little book and reread it, and found a description of that journey into darkness and reemergence into light and delight. It's a true story that wrote itself years before it happened.

Now, after living the story, I recognize the message of La Fille: More light, being in nature, body movement, and willingness to risk failure are valuable tools for finding the path out of darkness.

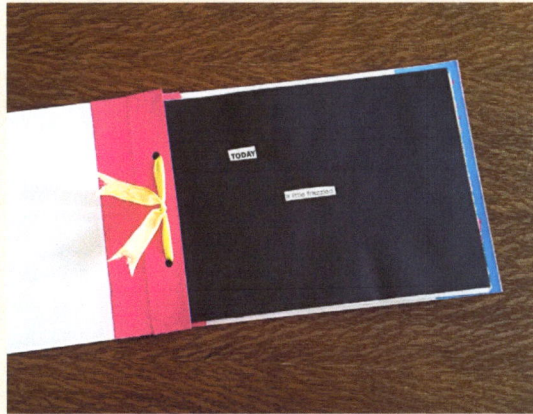

—GJH

the END

www.ingramcontent.com/pod-product-compliance
Lightning Source LLC
LaVergne TN
LVHW072104070426
835508LV00003B/255